Confucius Says...

Confucius Says…

By James Clum

James Clum

ISBN 978-1-300-59493-2

1sr Edition

Published by Lulu

Introduction

This book was written to inspire children to take an interest in world cultures and literature. In addition, it was my intention to encourage children to interpret language creatively in their own words. Beyond the academic side of the book, I was interested in engaging students in a dialogue about character. Getting students to think and discuss things like character, virtues, and ethics is not easy. It requires that students really open up and express how they feel.

So why Confucius? This is the first book of what will be a series on historical philosophers and thinkers. This provides the classroom teacher with the ability to add depth and complexity to their lessons by teaching across the various academic disciplines while at the same time providing stimulating ideas for discussion that will facilitate a deeper understanding of content.

I have selected quotes by Confucius from perhaps his most famous work, *Analects*. These words were originally translated by James Legge from his book, *Chinese Classics* which was written in 1891. The quotes presented here were chosen for their simplicity. Therefore, by repeating them students are encouraged to listen more carefully, summarize and paraphrase. Children may come to their own conclusions about the real value of what they hear, and this can only be done, in my opinion, by personal reflection and social interaction.

It is suggested that one read this book to students a little at a time. It was written for students Grades 4-7. Rather than explaining Confucius to them, it would be better to let children tell you what they think it is about. Their insights will surprise you. The book is set up in a particular pattern that will establish a routine that children will become familiar with. This will help to keep the short lessons on track. First, a little introduction to each topic is provided that will provide a context to the content that is given. Next, a quote by Confucius is shown that is short enough that students will be able to follow along with. As a teacher, try to encourage students to listen carefully the first time, only repeat as necessary.

Each topic has a few questions for discussion. Begin the discussion by asking, "Any ideas?" In this way, you can encourage students to initiate conversation on their own rather than having to prompt them with a specific question. Of course in a classroom setting, there will always be a select group of students who frequently raise their hands. I would however try to randomly call on students. By doing so, everyone will feel compelled to listen more attentively. Try not to give hints. If students hit a roadblock, have them get out of it by asking you the teacher questions with yes or no answers until they can proceed. You can also have students who demonstrate a deeper understanding of the material to help explain certain things to others students who are having trouble.

This book is intended to get students excited and engaged. Classroom discussions will become more lively if students are encouraged to disagree with others when they feel strongly about something. Though it may seem that you are promoting conflict; in reality, one is drawing out honesty. This material can be difficult at times, but through difficulty comes a sense of accomplishment.

1. The Life of Confucius

Confucius is considered one of the greatest teachers that has ever lived. Although he was born in China around 551-479 BCE, his words have spread all over the world and his ideas have had a major influence on Japanese, Korean and Vietnamese cultures. Here is the first of many quotes. It is Confucius as an old man reflecting on his life. Listen carefully...

> "Confucius said, 'At fifteen, I had my mind bent on learning.
>
> 'At thirty, I stood firm.
>
> 'At forty, I had no doubts.
>
> 'At fifty, I knew the decrees of Heaven.
>
> 'At sixty, my ear was an obedient organ for the reception of truth.
>
> 'At seventy, I could follow what my heart desired, without transgressing what was right.'

Discussion

What do you think the quote is about? (Give students a few moments before and after asking questions.)

Confucius seems to be talking about how his life has changed over time. He is summarizing his life and how his thinking has changed at every stage.

What have been the stages of your own life?

How has the way you thought about life changed as you have gotten older?

Confucius

2. Knowing Others

Let's take a look at another quote...

> Confucius said, 'I will not be afflicted at men's not knowing me; I will be afflicted that I do not know men.'

Any ideas?

Let's read it again, and this time, let's change the word "afflicted" to "hurt by."

> Confucius said, 'I will not be hurt by men not knowing me; I will be hurt by not knowing men.'

Discussion

Any ideas?

Do you think Confucius is only talking about men and not women, too?

What could we substitute for the word "men" in this quote?

Why is it not important that everybody knows who you are?

Why is it more important to know others than to worry about whether or not they know you?

How do you think Confucius felt about being famous?

3. Knowing Others

Confucius believed that people are all born essentially the same. As we get older we make decisions that change the paths of our lives and we become different from each other. He believed that having a good character was more important than all the riches in the world. Having a good character is something that we can all work on.

Let's take a look at another quote...

> Confucius said, 'What the wise man seeks is in his self. What the average man seeks is in others.'

Discussion

Any ideas?

Be honest and trustworthy are examples of virtues. Can you think of other virtues that someone who has good character has?

Is it ever too late to change one's character? Why or Why not?

What kind of things do people look for in other people that they want?

Do you think each person has inside themselves the things that would make them truly happy? Why or Why not?

Do things really make people happy?

Is happiness a choice?

4. Judging the Words of Others

Confucius believed that we should not like people just because of what they say, nor dislike what people say just because of whom people are.

Let's take a look at another quote...

> Confucius said, 'The wise man does not promote a man simply on account of his words, nor does he put aside good words because of the man.'

Discussion

Any ideas?

What does it mean "promote a man?"

What word could we replace "on account of" with?

Can you think of anyone famous people that many others listen to just because of who they are?

Why should a person listen to the value of other people's words and not think of whether or not they like that person?

Can you share a time in your life when you just wouldn't listen to someone, no matter what they said, just because you were upset with them?

Give some examples of how grownups do this.

5. Showing Humility

Confucius believed that people should work hard on being the best that they can be at whatever they choose to do. More than likely Confucius would not take credit for his successes. It seems that he would probably owe his success to hard work or the help of others.

Let's look at another quote...

> Confucius said, 'He who speaks without modesty will find it difficult to make his words good.'

Discussion

Any ideas?

What does Confucius mean by modesty?

Can you give some examples of being modest?

One someone finishes something really great, what should they say if someone compliments them?

Why is it hard for people to be humble when they are praised for doing something good?

Why is being humble important?

Explain what you think Confucius meant when he said that the person would "find it difficult to make his words good."

6. Following Rules and Laws

Confucius believed that people in communities, cities, states and even countries would live better in harmony together if everybody followed the laws. He believed that by following laws everything would run more smoothly.

Let's look at another quote...

> Confucius said, 'The wise man thinks of virtue; the small man thinks of comfort. The wise man thinks of the enforcement of law; the small man thinks of favors which he may receive.'

Discussion

Any ideas?

What do you think Confucius means by a "small man?"

What are some laws that people break just because it is more convenient for them?

What would happen if nobody followed the rules while driving?

Why do we need laws?

Can you think of some examples of rules in the classroom that students break just because they think that they will get away with it?

Why do we need rules in the classroom?

Do you think Confucius would jaywalk if he were late for a meeting and walking around in New York City? What do you think about this?

7. Having Faults

Confucius is considered a Chinese sage or "wise person." Perhaps more than any other sage of his time or since, he emphasized the importance of conduct. By this I mean that he thought that people's behavior in general was extremely important. Since nobody is perfect, he believed that it is the responsibility of each person to realize his or her problems, and try to do something to correct them. To not see the problems in oneself, in the eyes of Confucius, is an even bigger problem.

Let's look at another quote...

> Confucius said, 'To have faults and not to reform them,-- this, indeed, should be pronounced having faults.'

Discussion

Any Ideas?

What does Confucius mean by" faults?"

Greediness and Stinginess are examples of faults. Can you give some more examples of common faults people have?

What does he mean by "reform" them?

Why is it difficult for people to get rid of their faults?

Why is it better to look at our own faults rather than point out the faults of others?

8. Giving Advice

Since we have already discussed that Confucius thinks everyone should worry about their own faults and not the faults of others, it is no surprise that Confucius would advise people to mind their own business. Every person's life is a unique journey. When we look at someone else's problem and say that she should do this or that, we are judging this person from our own perspective.

Let's look at another quote...

> Confucius said, 'Those whose courses are different cannot lay plans for one another.'

See if you can reword this quote in your own words to capture what Confucius meant. If you need to, we can read it again.

Discussion

Any ideas?

When you have a problem that is really upsetting, which do you prefer: people who just listen to you or people who give you good advice? There is no right answer so please just explain which you prefer and explain why.

Do you think most people feel the same way?

Explain

9. The Love of Comfort

Sometimes people might look at the writing of Confucius and come to the conclusion that he thought some people were better than others. This however, is not true. Confucius valued certain qualities in others. The qualities that he cherished were qualities that the person worked hard to achieve. They were not material things like money or valued personal things, but rather virtues such as kindness, and wisdom that the person developed from learning about life.

Let's look at another quote...

> Confucius said, 'The scholar who cherishes the love of comfort is not fit to be deemed a scholar.'

See if you can reword this quote in your own words to capture what Confucius meant. If you need to, we can read it again.

Discussion

Any ideas?

What do you think Confucius valued more: things or ideas? Explain why using the actual quote or your paraphrasing of it.

What are some things that you have already learned about Confucius that help you to come to this conclusion?

10. Encouraging Others

Confucius was famous in his own lifetime. He was regarded by other scholars as being wise and many people came to him for advice. According to Confucius, it one's duty and obligation to help others become recognized for their talents and successes once a person has become famous. Even if one has not become successful yet, by making others greater, we in turn can become greater.

Let's look at another quote...

> 'Now the man of perfect virtue, wishing to be established himself, seeks also to establish others; wishing to be enlarged himself, he seeks also to enlarge others.

Discussion

Any ideas?

What does Confucius mean by "establishing himself?"

What are some things that you could say about a friend's hobbies that would make them feel "bigger" about themselves.

What happens to people when they don't receive encouragement?

Who would like to share a time when someone gave you encouragement that helped you to go on when you felt like giving up?

Which feels better: being complimented on your effort or your intelligence? Explain why.

11. Simple Living

According to Confucius, he doesn't need a whole lot to be happy because the pleasures of this world do not last. Though Confucius does not have much in the way of material possessions, he is happy with the knowledge that is a good person on the inside. This is worth more to him than external wealth. His treasure is found inside.

Let's look at another quote...

> Confucius said, 'With coarse rice to eat, with water to drink, and my bended arm for a pillow; I have still joy in the midst of these things. Riches and honors acquired by unrighteous means are to me as a floating cloud.'

Discussion

Any ideas?

What is the main idea of this quote?

Using what you read from the quote, justify your opinion.

Let's imagine that you were Confucius. Based on just this quote what would be your biggest fear in life?

What do you think Confucius considered as his priorities?

Do you agree or disagree with his priorities? Explain why.

12. Being Smart

Confucius has been the model teacher all over Asia for over a thousand years. On Confucius birthday which is September 28th, people in some parts of Asia present their teachers with a gift of gratitude. So, people might think that Confucius was a really smart guy. A teacher's teacher you might say.

Let's look at another quote...

> Confucius said, 'I am not one who was born in the possession of knowledge; I am one who is fond of antiquity, and earnest in seeking it there.'

Here's one way to paraphrase the quote...

> I wasn't born smart. I got that way because I worked hard at my love of history.

Discussion

Any ideas?

According to the quote, how did Confucius become wise?

Look at this statement...Praise others for their efforts and not their intelligence.

Do you agree or disagree with this statement. Explain why.

What is the overall effect of praising others for their intelligence rather than their hard work?

13. Keeping Your Head

I bet if Confucius sat next to you on the bus, he would be a very pleasant person to talk to. He would show manners and ask you politely what your name is. I think he would ask about your family and your favorite subjects in school. If the bus suddenly had an accident, I think he would probably keep his cool. How about you?

Listen to responses...

Let's look at another quote...

> Confucius said, 'The wise man is satisfied and composed; the average man is always full of distress.'

Discussion

Any ideas?

Which word in the quote means "keeping your cool?"

Why do average people get upset easily over small things?

Do you think Confucius got upset over small things like everybody else or do you think that he was just making this up?

What would make Confucius hard to live with?

Do you think Confucius was an introvert or an extrovert? Explain why.

Assignment 1

Creative Writing- Confucius Has Culture Shock

Purpose:

Students will use their imaginations to describe the difficulties that Confucius would experience in the modern world. This will demonstrate a keen understanding of certain historical, cultural and philosophical differences that demonstrate a deeper understanding of Confucius.

Assignment:

Students are assigned a creative writing assignment using the title above or a similar title of their own choosing. The paper should be a minimum of one page front and back.

Correct indentation, grammar, and spelling are required as always.

Students must use quoted speech within the story.

Assignment 2

Interview- Confucius on the Tonight Show

Purpose:

Students will use their imagination to represent how Confucius and Jay Leno would talk to each other based on their personalities. This lesson will encourage students to demonstrate their knowledge of Confucius while at the same time representing an informative and interesting dialogue.

Assignment:

Students will write a script for two characters: Confucius and Jay Leno. As a host, Jay Leno will ask engaging questions to Confucius regarding topics of the student's choice. These questions may ask about his life, interests, opinions or other topics of interest.

The script must be at least one page front and back in length.

Students will be asked to perform their scripts in front of the class in an environment that is set up to resemble a show.

Assignment 3

Role Play-Confucius is the Assistant Principle

Purpose:

Students will demonstrate their knowledge of how Confucius might interact with kids in a school environment especially with regards to the importance of personal conduct. In addition, students will approach this challenging exercise in a lighthearted way.

Assignment:

Students are provided with the following situation...

A boy has been sent to Assistant Principal Confucius for counseling. The boy was caught cheating on a test. The boy admits that he wrote the answers down to the questions on his arm with a pen. He is now in the office.

Students are not given time to prepare what they are going to say. Each must come up and role-play the situation.

Each segment should be about 3 minutes in length.

Props will be set up to create an environment similar to an office.

Assignment 4

Personal Letter-Confucius Write a Letter to the President

Purpose:

Students will demonstrate their understanding of Confucius' views on human conduct. Students will additionally demonstrate their understanding of how to properly write a personal letter in the correct format.

Assignment:

Students will write a letter neatly by hand in cursive using the correct format of a personal letter.

Attention must be paid to correct indentation, grammar and spelling.

Attention must be paid to having an introduction, body and closing.

Assignment 5

Listening Activity-Chinese Whispers

Purpose:

Students will demonstrate their ability to listen carefully and repeat what they hear.

Assignment:

The teacher will select one of the quotes in this book and whisper it into the ear of a student. That student will whisper the quote to another student. Each student who hears the quote will again whisper it to someone else so that the quote is circulated quietly throughout the room. At some point the teacher will ask the last student to repeat the quote. Different quotes can be used, and it is up to the teacher's discretion to determine when the quote should be repeated aloud.

Assignment 6

Brainstorming-Confucius

Purpose:

Students will brainstorm vocabulary words related to Confucius in order to demonstrate that they can quickly access the topic in their thoughts.

Assignment:

Students will be given 10 minutes to come up with as many single words as they can related to Confucius. These words can be nouns, verbs, or adjectives.

Students will write these words down as a list.

The goal is to come up with as many correctly spelled words as possible.

Students will share their lists with the other students surrounding them once the time limit is reached.

As students here additional words, they will add these words to their own lists.

Students will then share their words with the class.

The winner with the most words gets a prize.

Assignment 7

Cluster Diagram- Confucius

Purpose:

Students will organize and prioritize the vocabulary list that was developed from Assignment 6.

Assignment:

Students will develop a cluster diagram that groups words from the vocabulary list produced in Assignment 6 according to various topics related to Confucius.

The center oval of the cluster diagram should say Confucius.

Ovals surrounding the center oval should reflect how the list can be divided up into categories.

A minimum of 60 ovals is required.

Ovals should be numbered.

Assignment 8

Research- Confucius Biography

Purpose:

Students will use and develop their research skills by going to the library and finding out more information about Confucius.

Assignment:

Students will research one of the following topics in the library:

Biography of Confucius

Political Views of Confucius

Impact of Confucianism on Chinese Culture

Students will take notes from various resources or print the resources that they deem important.

Students will then be given the task of writing a one page front and back essay on their findings.

Students must include at least three references in a bibliography.

A Gifted Education

is not just for the Gifted.

Notes

Bibliography

The English text of the translation is derived from "The Chinese Classics, Volume I: Confucian Analects" by James Legge, 1891.

The website YellowBridge was used as a reference.

http://www.yellowbridge.com/onlinelit/analects.php

Made in the USA
Las Vegas, NV
12 November 2020